First published in Great Britain in 1996 by Brockhampton Press,
a member of the Hodder Headline Group,
20 Bloomsbury Street, London WC1B 3QA.

This series of little gift books was made by Frances Banfield,
Kate Brown, Laurel Clark, Penny Clarke, Clive Collins, Melanie
Cumming, Nick Diggory, Deborah Gill, David Goodman, Douglas
Hall, Maureen Hill, Nick Hutchison, John Hybert, Kate Hybert,
Douglas Ingram, Simon London, Patrick McCreeth, Morse Modaberi,
Tara Neill, Anne Newman, Grant Oliver, Michelle Rogers,
Nigel Soper, Karen Sullivan and Nick Wells.

ISBN 1 86019 463 X
A copy of the CIP data is available from the
British Library upon request.

Produced for Brockhampton Press by Flame Tree Publishing,
part of The Foundry Creative Media Company Limited,
The Long House, Antrobus Road, Chiswick W4 5HY.

Printed and bound in Italy by L.E.G.O. Spa.

The Funny Book of
SOCCER

Words selected by
Bob Hale

Cartoons by

Football's a game of skill ... we kicked
them a bit and they kicked us a bit.
Graham Roberts

It's a renaissance - or, put more simply,
some you win, some you lose.
Desmond Lynam

So that's 1-0, sounds like the score at
Boundary Park where of course it's 2-2.
Jack Wainwright

I am a firm believer that if you score one goal
the other team have to score two to win.
Howard Wilkinson

'Ello, 'ello - it's spread to the director's box.

If you had to name one particular person
to blame it would have to be the players.
Theo Foley

Dickie Davies: What's he going to be
telling his team at half-time, Denis?
Denis Law: He'll be telling them that
there are 45 minutes left to play ...

After a goalless first half, the
score at half-time is 0-0.
Brian Moore

The last player to score a hat trick in a cup
final was Stan Mortenson. He even had a
final named after him - the Matthews final.
Lawrie McMenemy

I didn't take drugs and above all I did
not let down those who love me.
*Diego Maradona, on having been expelled from
the World Cup for taking drugs, 1994*

•

"Nice shot, but we changed ends at half-time...remember?"

"He's the most conscientious
groundsman we've ever had."

Some of these players never dreamed they'd be
playing in a Cup Final at Wembley - but here
they are today, fulfilling those dreams.
Lawrie McMenemy

Sporting Lisbon in their green and white
hooped shirts ... they look like a team of zebras.
Peter Jones

My left foot is not one of my best.
Sammy McIlroy

And now, the familiar sight of Liverpool
raising the League Cup for the first time.
Brian Moore

It's been an amazing year for Crystal Palace
over the last 12 months ...
Brian Moore

"Effective, yes – but not in the rule book, I fear."

With the very last kick of the game, Bobby
McDonald scored with a header.

Alan Parry

I don't think, Brian.
You don't think in this game.

Allan Clarke

And Ritchie has now scored 11 goals,
exactly double the number he scored last season.

Alan Parry

My father was a miner and he
worked down a mine.

Kevin Keegan

Hollins, of course, never believes that a match has finished until the final whistle has blown.

Peter Jones

Suddenly a Tommy came with a football, kicking already and making fun, and then began a football match. We marked the goals with our caps. Teams were quickly established for a match on the frozen mud, and the Fritzes beat the Tommies 3-2.

Lieutenant Johannes Niemann (133rd Saxon Regt), first-hand account of a football game which took place between the opposing armies on the Western Front on Christmas Day, 1914

The Spaniards have been reduced to aiming aimless balls into the goal.

Ron Atkinson

"...so you've not played recently..?"

*"But surely you can't all have important
business meetings during the match?"*

I felt a lump in my mouth as the ball went in.

Terry Venables

You won't find too many Hollywood producers
and West End theatre impresarios sneering
at the public's desire to be diverted, so why
should football managers get away with it?

Nick Hornby, **Fever Pitch**

Football hooliganism is not a British disease.
We simply perfected it.

Laurie Graham, **The British Abroad**

Footballers are the game's fodder, human
sacrifices that are thrown without sentiment
or apologies into the battlefield.

Hunter Davies, **A Footballer's Lot**

Climate, temperament, history - all of
these contribute to style, which is an
aspect of character, individual or national.

Terence Delaney, **Boys in the Park**

And now, International Soccer Special:
Manchester United v Southampton.

David Coleman

From as far back as I remember I have kicked a
ball. Even when it was with just a collection of
old rags tied together, it became a big match.
It took the importance of the international stage.
The cameras were there, there was the build-up,
the team talk, and the tactics, which were always,

Attack! Attack! Attack!

Richard Johnson, **The Trial**

"You'll have to move your car, lad – you're parked in the chairman's space..."

At the international level, sport
is frankly mimic warfare.
George Orwell, **The Sporting Spirits**

❧

REFEREE: A few pearls of wisdom. From
one who knows ... what we're now about to
witness is called a football match. Not the
beginning of World War III. Not the
destruction of the human race. A football match.
Jack Rosenthal, **Sunday Morning**

❧

To some, football ...
In the sadness of an autumn afternoon
studs and mud the memorable dribble ...
Alan Ross, **Boyhood**

"They're forecasting a big gate today, so stay close..."

"Hang on, lads...it's getting quite exciting..."

The ball jumped up and out and hung on the wind
Over a gulf of treetops.
Then they all shouted together, and the
ball blew back.
Ted Hughes, **Football at Slack**

The goals made such a difference
to the way this game went.
John Motson

Football is not just kicking a ball about
and hoping it goes in the right direction.
It's a science, an art form, a subject to study
just like maths, chemistry, or history.
Paul Gascoigne, **Soccer Skills with Gazza**

... It's like the old gag about the football team who are brilliant on paper but crap on grass ...

*Bruce Dessau, **Writing About Comedy***

The natural state of the football fan is bitter disappointment, no matter what the score.

*Nick Hornby, **Fever Pitch***

I've never actually met a football player but Match of the Day is an absolute godsend. It's the only time you will have free to wash your hair, or pluck your eyebrows - your man will be absolutely glued to the box. Watch out for Action Replays, though.

*Jilly Cooper, **Men and Super Men***

Plenty of goals in Divisions Three and Four today. Darlington nil, Hereford nil.

Commentator, Radio 2

"Only a game? Who on earth has been filling your head with all that rubbish?"

Football isn't a matter of life and death -
it's much more important than that.
Bill Shankly

Oh he's football crazy, he's football mad
And the football it has robbed him o'
the wee bit sense he had.
Roger McGough, **Jimmy McGregor**

We should give the game back to the
players; they've had everything else.
Ron Atkinson

I would have given my right arm
to have been a pianist.
Bobby Robson

"*There's a nasty rumour going round that you've accepted a bribe...*"

"Oh Lor'...he's going to give us one of his half-time pep talks!"

Alcoholism v Communism
Banner at Scotland v Soviet Union game

They are a strange looking people.
They wear Union Jacks and tattoos, but
some of them are really quite nice.
British Consul in Bilbao on England fans

I'm one of a dying breed -
a Chelsea season-ticket holder.
Dennis Waterman

In some respects soccer is a bit like the
dinosaur. You give it a kick up the backside
and three years later its head drops off.
Ron Jones

Vocabulary – tha's my biggest failing. I try very hard to think of something clever or witty to say when a ball goes into the net but I usually end up saying, 'Oh, what a goal!'

John Motson, football commentator

Our methods are so easy, sometimes players don't understand them at first.

Joe Fagan, Liverpool manager 1983

I always remember after a dull Cup Final at Wembley, I was escorting the Queen to her car and I said: 'Did you think anyone played well today, ma'am?' and she said: 'Yes, the band.'

Sir Stanley Rous on his days as FA secretary

If you want to win football games, you've got to score goals.

Graham Taylor

"It's the pressure of knowing that someone's pools jackpot could rest on my skill in goal."

I don't watch television myself but my family do, and they tell me that the most popular programmes are the ones which are full of violence. On that basis football ought to do rather well.

Jack Dunnett, chairman of the Football League, 1985

I'd rather have a guy take me to a football match and have a drink afterwards than to go to bed with someone.

Samantha Fox

Wembley is beginning to blacken with people in terms of red and blue.

Alan Jackson

He gets great elevation on his balls.

David Pleat, on Maradona

"Well it's not my idea of being on the transfer list..."

"It's not fair – you took that shot while I wasn't looking..."

I've had to swap my Merc for a BMW,
I'm down to my last 37 suits and I'm
drinking non-vintage champagne.
Ron Atkinson, after his dismissal as
Manchester United manager 1987

In my day there were plenty of footballers
around who would kick your bollocks off.
The difference was that at the end they would
shake your hand and help you look for them.
Nat Lofthouse

The only thing Norwich didn't get
was the goal that they finally got.
Jimmy Greaves

"I just don't know why I joined this club – the strip does nothing for my complexion at all!"

... Nothing but beastly fury and extreme violence,
whereof proceedeth hurt; and consequently rancour
and malice do remain with them that be wounded.

Thomas Elyot, 15th century

Football hooligans? Well there are
92 club chairmen for a start.

Brian Clough

We've got a long-term plan at this club
and except for the results it's going well.

Ernie Clay

It's Great Britain in the all-white strip,
with the red and blue V, the dark
shorts and the dark stockings.

Ray French

A footballer died and arrived at the gates of heaven where an angel awaited him. 'Now,' said the angel, 'before you enter here, is there anything that happened to you on earth upon which you would like your mind set at rest?'

The footballer thought for a moment and then said: 'There is one matter, I belonged to the famous St Mirren Club and one cup final when we were playing the Rangers, I scored a goal which I am sure was off-side. It won us the match and the cup, but I've always been troubled about it.'

'Oh,' replied the angel, 'we know all about the goal up here. It was perfectly right, so you can banish all your doubts.'

'Oh, thank you, St Peter,' said the footballer.

The angel replied: 'But I'm not St Peter, you know.'

'Then who are you?' asked the footballer.

'St Mirren,' came the reply.

Commentator, Radio 2

"Never mind the coin – help me find my contact lens..."

The goal stands up, the keeper
Stands up to keep the goal.
*A.E. Housman, **A Shropshire Lad***

It's now 4-3 to Oldham.
The goals are going in like dominoes.
Commentator, Piccadilly Radio

Coventry City were sixth in the First Division when
they decided to send their star players to ballet
school. The coach decided that graceful exercises to
the 'Dance of the Sugar Plum Fairy' might improve
their coordination. The team who were more used
to passes than pas-de-deux, and preferred late
kick-offs to leotards, appeared
to take it stoically enough. The fans, however,
made it pretty clear what they thought about it
all on the terraces the following Saturday.
*Martyn Lewis, **News at Ten***

There are more hooligans in the House
of Commons than at a football match.
Brian Clough

An Italian 4th Division side – losing regularly
in home matches – decided on a drastic remedy.
The Borgosesia Manager called in the parish
priest to exorcise the pitch after fans complained
that only ghosts could have caused the town
to lose five games in a row. I suppose no-one
thought of blaming the players.
*Martyn Lewis, **News at Ten***

Watching football on TV is like
peeping through a keyhole.
Ron Greenwood

If God had wanted football to be played in the
air, he wouldn't have put grass on the ground.

Brian Clough

They are hanging out their jackets, and all who
mean real work, their hats, waistcoats, neck-
handkerchiefs, and braces, on the railings ...

Thomas Hughes, **Tom Brown's School Days**

A football coach is a man whose job is to
predict what will happen on Sunday
... then explain, on Monday, why it didn't.

Jeff Rovin, **1001 Great Sports Jokes**

We go into the second half with United
1-0 up, so the game is perfectly balanced.

Peter Jones

Ian Rush: Deadly ten times out of ten.
But that wasn't one of them.

Peter Jones

•

In the first-ever World Cup, the trainer of the
American soccer team set an example which no
other has yet managed to equal. In the 1930
semi-final Argentina had just scored a disputed
goal against the USA. Shouting abuse at the
referee as he travelled, our fellow dashed out
to tend an injured player. The 80,000-strong
crowd roared with approval as he ran on to the
pitch, threw down his medical bag, broke a bottle
of chloroform and anaesthetized himself.

He was carried off by his own team.

Stephen Pile, **The Return of Heroic Failures**

My son has the makings of a football hooligan:
he threw a bottle at the referee yesterday.
I wouldn't mind, but he broke the screen.

FOR SALE

A FEE WILL BE CHARGED FOR VIEWING THE UPSTAIRS DURING HOME GAMES

He's never been much of a sportsman.
They used to call him Cinderella in the
football team ... he kept missing the ball.

It slid away from his left boot, which
was poised with the trigger cocked.

Barry Davies

In winter football is a useful and charming
exercise. It is a leather ball about as big as
one's head, filled with wind. This kick'd about
from one to t'other end in the streets, by
him that can get it, and that is all the art of it.

François Mission, 1697

He hit the post, and after the game
people will say, well he hit the post.

Jimmy Greaves

The goal was scored a little bit by the hand of
God and a little bit by the head of Maradona.

*Diego Maradona, referring to the goal he scored
against England in the 1986 World Cup quarter final;
although scored illegally with the hand the referee
allowed it to stand*

<u>Football:</u> running 50 metres to kick a ball behind
two goalposts.

<u>Association Football:</u> running 50 metres to hit the
ball with your head behind two goalposts.

<u>Australian Rules Football:</u> running 50 metres to hit
the other player in the head from behind
two goalposts.

<u>Rugby League Football:</u> running 50 metres, getting
kicked in the behind, ramming the other player's
head into the goalposts and sod the ball.

*Colin Bowles, **The Wit's Dictionary***

COUNSELL
SERVIC

51

"Well, I think you could have tried a little harder to find a sitter during an away match!"

The devil was constantly challenging St Peter to a game of soccer, but St Peter refused, until one day while walking around heaven he discovered that quite a number of Irish international footballers had entered the 'pearly gates'.

'Now I'll arrange to play you that soccer game.' said St Peter. 'How about it?'

'You'll lose,' said the devil, 'you'll lose.'

'Oh, don't be sure,' replied St Peter.

'We now have in heaven a great number of international soccer stars from which to select a winning team.'

'You'll lose, you'll lose!' repeated the devil.

'What makes you so sure we'll lose?' enquired St Peter.

'Because,' laughed the devil, 'we have all the referees down here.'

Lord Blease, **Pass The Port Again**

Everything in our favour was against us.

Danny Blanchflower

No one, in fact, dies in *Psychic News*, they are always described as 'passing quietly to the other side', like crooked footballers ...

Jilly Cooper, **SuperJilly**

Then there was the football coach who decided to take a gorilla on tour with his team. So if any of his players got injured, he'd have spare parts.

Jeff Rovin, **1001 Great Sports Jokes**

Football's football: if that weren't the case it wouldn't be the game that it is.

Garth Crooks

For when the One Great Scorer comes
To write against your name,
He marks - not that you won or lost
But how you played the Game.
Grantland Rice, US sports writer 'Alumnus Football'

In England, soccer is a grey game
played by grey people on grey days.
Rodney Marsh

Being a woman is of special interest only to
aspiring male transsexuals. To actual women,
it is merely a good excuse not to play football.
Fran Lebowitz, **Metropolitan Life**

[Gary Lineker is] the Queen Mother of Football.
Arthur Smith and Chris England,
An Evening With Gary Lineker

"...So do they all come on to the field in ascending order of transfer fee..?"

If I had the wings of a sparrow
If I had the arse of a crow
I'd fly over Tottenham tomorrow
And shit on the bastards below.

Anonymous, **Chelsea Terraces**

I do love cricket - it's so very English.

Sarah Bernhardt, on seeing a game of football

We didn't underestimate them.
They were a lot better than we thought.

Bobby Robson, on Cameroon's football team, 1990

The streets were full of footballs.

Samuel Pepys, Diary, 1665

Football ... causeth fighting, brawling, contention, quarrel picking, murder, homicide and great effusion of bloode, as daily experience teacheth.

Philip Stubbes, **Anatomie of Abuses,** *1585*

George Best was often told by Matt Busby not to bother to turn up for Busby's team talks to Manchester United:
It wasn't worth his coming. It was a very simple team talk, All I used to say was: 'When ever possible, give the ball to George.'

Matt Busby, in Michael Parkinson, **Sporting Lives**

A man who had missed the last home match of United had to enter social life on tiptoe in Bruddersford.

J.B. Preistley, **The Good Companions**

"It's OK - I'm in BUPA!"

Our company only sponsors the arts. I don't
think Stenhousemuir could be regarded by
any stretch of the imagination as artistic.
*Anonymous reply by a Prudential Insurance public relations
officer when fans asked for sponsorship, following a
series of advertisements featuring Stenhousemuir*

The great fallacy is that the game is first and last
about winning. It's nothing of the kind. The game
is about glory. It's about doing things in style,
with a flourish, about going out and beating the
other lot, not waiting for them to die of boredom.
Danny Blanchflower, in Hunter Davies, **The Glory Game**

One of the secrets of football
is the simplicity of its laws.
Joseph Blatter, FIFA Secretary

Acknowledgements:

The Publishers wish to thank everyone who gave permission to reproduce the quotes in this book. Every effort has been made to contact the copyright holders, but in the event that an oversight has occurred, the publishers would be delighted to rectify any omissions in future editions of this book. *Classic Sports Quotes*, Peter Ball and Phil Shaw, Chancellor Press; *5000 One- and Two-Line Jokes*, Leopold Fechtner, Thorson's; *The Huge Joke Book*, Goldstein, Jackson, Ford and Newman, Random House Inc.; *Murphy's Law*, Arthur Bloch, reprinted courtesy of Methuen, London; *And Finally ...*, Martyn Lewis, reprinted courtesy of Hutchinson, part of Random House; *The Random House Book of Jokes and Anecdotes*, Joe Claro, reprinted courtesy of Random House Inc.; *Just Say a Few Words*, Bob Monkhouse, reprinted courtesy of Arrow Books, part of Random House UK Ltd.